BOULDER CITY LIBRARY

3 1432 00129 6530

D1627223

J
937
.7
LIN

Lindeen, Mary

Ashes to ashes: uncovering Pompeii

Boulder City Library
701 Adams Boulevard
Boulder City, NV 89005

Uncovering Pompeii

© 2008 Weldon Owen Education Inc. All rights reserved.

No part of this publication may be reproduced or transmitted
in any form or by any means, electronic or mechanical,
including photocopying, recording, taping, or any information storage
and retrieval system, without permission in writing from the publisher.

Library of Congress Cataloging-in-Publication Data

Lindeen, Mary.
   Ashes to ashes : uncovering Pompeii / Mary Lindeen.
       p. cm. -- (Shockwave)
   Includes index.
   ISBN-10: 0-531-17745-9 (lib. bdg.)
   ISBN-13: 978-0-531-17745-7 (lib. bdg.)
   ISBN-10: 0-531-15544-7 (pbk.)
   ISBN-13: 978-0-531-15544-8 (pbk.)
1. Pompeii (Extinct city)--Juvenile literature. 2. Vesuvius
(Italy)--Eruption, 79--Juvenile literature. 3. Excavations
(Archaeology)--Italy--Pompeii (Extinct city)--Juvenile literature.
I. Title. II. Series.

   DG70.P7L48 2007
   937'.7--dc22

2007012222

Published in 2008 by Children's Press, an imprint of Scholastic Inc.,
557 Broadway, New York, New York 10012
www.scholastic.com

SCHOLASTIC, CHILDREN'S PRESS, and associated logos are trademarks
and/or registered trademarks of Scholastic Inc.

08 09 10 11 12 13 14 15 16 17
10 9 8 7 6 5 4 3 2 1

Printed in China through Colorcraft Ltd., Hong Kong

Author: Mary Lindeen
Educational Consultant: Ian Morrison
Editor: Janine Scott
Designer: Amy Lam
Photo Researchers: Jamshed Mistry and Sarah Matthewson
Illustrations by: Amy Lam (pp. 11, 13, 14, 23)

Photographs by: Capware: RAS Foundation/www.stabiae.org (Villa San Marco,
pp. 28–29); **Getty Images** (illustration of public square, pp. 12–13; repairing damage,
p. 21; gladiators, p. 25); **Jennifer and Brian Lupton** (teenagers, pp. 32–33); **Photodisc**
(eruption, p. 13); **Photolibrary** (pp. 8–9; stepping stones, p. 11; pp. 14–15; gladiator's
helmet, p. 25; boat chamber, p. 27); **Stockxpert** (Vesuvius, pp. 32–33); **TopFoto/www.
stockcentral.co.nz** (dog warning, p. 19; Pompeii bread, p. 24; Stabiae fresco, p.29);
Tranz/Corbis (cover; p. 3; p. 7; p. 10; public bath, p. 11; pp. 16–18; gold lamp,
glassware, p. 19; p. 20; Giuseppe Fiorelli, p. 21; pp. 22–23; Roman oven, p. 24;
barracks, pp. 24–25; p. 26; Ring Lady, p. 27; pp. 30–31)

The publisher would like to thank Capware and Audrey Fastuca of the RAS Foundation
for providing the 3-D illustrations of the Villa San Marco on pp. 28–29.

All other illustrations and photographs © Weldon Owen Education Inc.

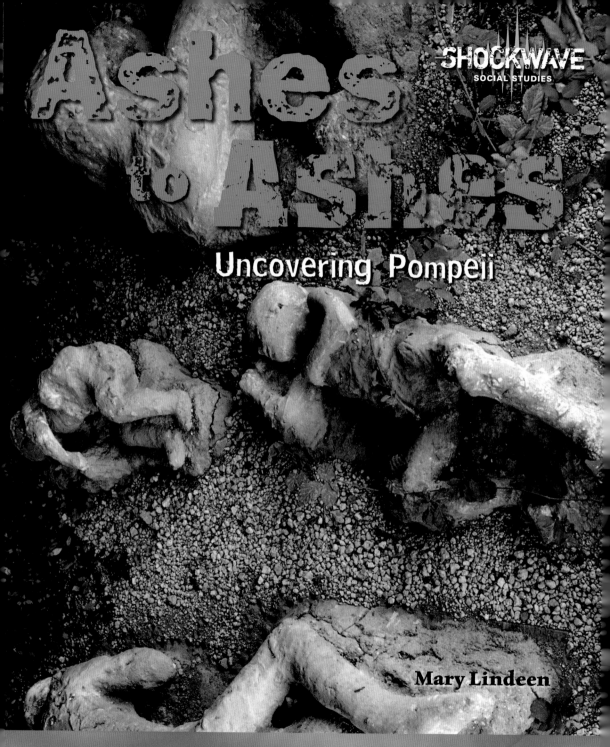

Ashes to Ashes

Uncovering Pompeii

Mary Lindeen

children's press®

An imprint of Scholastic Inc.

NEW YORK • TORONTO • LONDON • AUCKLAND • SYDNEY
MEXICO CITY • NEW DELHI • HONG KONG
DANBURY, CONNECTICUT

SHOCKWAVE
SOCIAL STUDIES

Boulder City Library
701 Adams Boulevard
Boulder City, NV 89005

JUN 2008

CHECK THESE OUT!

SHOCKER

Stuff to Shock,
Surprise, and
Amaze You

Quick Recaps
and Notable
Notes

Word Stunners
and Other Oddities

The Heads-Up
on Expert Reading

Links to More
Information

CONTENTS

archaeologist (*ar kee OL uh jist*) a scientist who studies people and objects from the past

artifact (*ART uh fakt*) an object from the past, such as a tool, that was made by humans

excavate (*EK skuh vate*) to dig down to reveal ancient ruins and remains

fresco (*FRESS koh*) a kind of painting done on wet plaster with water-based paint

mosaic (*moh ZAY ik*) a picture or pattern made up of different-colored pieces of tiles, stones, or gla

surge (*SURJ*) a cloud of gas and volcanic debris that moves rapidly

· ·

For additional vocabulary, see Glossary on page 34.

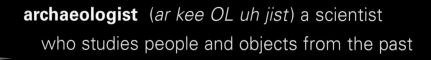

In words such as *archaeologist* and *archaeology*, *archaeo* means "relating to prehistoric times." The *ology* means "the study of" and *ologist* refers to the person who studies it.

The ancient Roman city of Pompeii (*Pahm PAY*) is like a time capsule. During the **eruption** of Mount Vesuvius (*Ve SU vee uhs*) in 79 A.D., Pompeii was buried under 13 feet of volcanic ash and rocks.

The first explosion happened at dawn on August 24th. Later that day, buildings started to collapse. People died trying to escape. Dogs died, still chained to their houses. The next morning, Pompeii lay silent. The city and its people lay hidden under ash. Then, more than 1,500 years later, the tragedy of Pompeii was discovered by accident.

Ruins at Pompeii

EUROPE

ITALY

ITALY

Misenum

Naples Herculaneum

Mount
Vesuvius

Gulf of
Naples

Pompeii

Stabiae

Mount Vesuvius

In the first century A.D., Pompeii was a lively seaside city. It was located near the Mediterranean Sea. About 20,000 people lived in Pompeii. Wealthy Romans flocked there to enjoy the sunny weather. Many owned vacation **villas** in Pompeii.

The city had much to offer. Its streets were lined with houses and shops. There were bakeries, butcher shops, laundries, and fast-food shops. There were even 118 bars!

The city center had an open square. This was called a forum. People shopped at a market held there. There were many large buildings around the forum. People went to concerts and plays at the theater. They watched **gladiator** fights at the **amphitheater**. They washed in the public baths.

Covered walkway

Frescoes

Bronze statue

Roman houses often wrapped around a garden and a courtyard. They had **frescoes** on the walls. They had **mosaics** on the floors. Some houses had bars over the windows. This was to stop robbers from entering.

SHOCKER

The public toilets were just that – public! People chatted as they sat on the toilet. They used olive oil and a wet sponge on a stick to wipe themselves!

Words ending in double consonants are quite common. Words such as *Pompeii* that end in double vowels are less common. Here are some examples: *baa, degree, cuckoo.*

Public bath

There were five public baths in Pompeii. Bathers would first have a cold bath in the cold room. Then they went to the warm room. There they were oiled. After that, they visited the hot room to sweat. They were also scraped clean. Next they took a hot bath. Then they went for a cold bath again.

The cobbled streets of Pompeii had raised sidewalks. Some streets had large stepping stones for crosswalks. These helped people keep their feet dry.

Cold Room: Frigidarium

Warm Room: Tepidarium

Hot Room: Caldarium

11

A Day of Death

The date was August 24, 79 A.D. At dawn, the people of Pompeii heard a small explosion from Mount Vesuvius. No one seemed too concerned. They went about their day as normal. However, soon that would all change. At 1:00 P.M., there was a massive explosion. The ground shook violently. Mount Vesuvius had just erupted. Hot volcanic ash and rocks fell down on the city. The sky grew as dark as night. The air contained poisonous gases.

The heading sounds like a headline, and the first paragraph sounds like a newspaper report. So I expect the next few pages will tell me what happened on that day.

The people of Pompeii knew something terrible had happened. They did not know that soon thousands of them would be dead. They did not know that their city was about to be buried for hundreds of years.

HOT STUFF!

Hot volcanic ash rained down on Pompeii. Volcanic ash is made up of fine fragments of rock. It is one of the greatest volcanic dangers. Ash can bury, burn, choke, and poison people, animals, and plants.

The rocks that fell on Pompeii were a kind called pumice. Pumice is a volcanic rock with many holes in it. The holes are created by gas bubbles. Pumice is very light.

Nowhere to Run

In the afternoon, the people of Pompeii grabbed their families and valuables. They ran for their lives. Some were killed by falling rocks. Many people made it to the beach. They wanted to escape in boats. However, the water soon became blocked with ash and rocks. Some people ran inside their homes and other buildings. The weight of the volcanic **debris** on the roofs made some buildings cave in. The people inside were crushed to death.

The rocks and ash kept falling. They covered everything. By the next day, the debris was more than 9 feet deep. At about 8 o'clock that morning, a final **surge** occurred. Super-hot ash, rocks, and deadly gases hit Pompeii. An hour later, Pompeii lay buried under about 13 feet of ash and rocks. There was nothing – and no one – left. The volcano lay quiet too.

Two Days in Pompeii

August 24

Dawn	1:00 P.M.	2:30 P.M.	5:00 P.M.
A small explosion occurs. A small column of ash and rock rises.	A huge explosion occurs. A large column of ash and rock rises nine miles into the sky.	The sky darkens. The earth trembles. The column of ash is 16 miles high.	Roofs collapse. Buildings shake. The people of Pompeii **evacuate**.

14

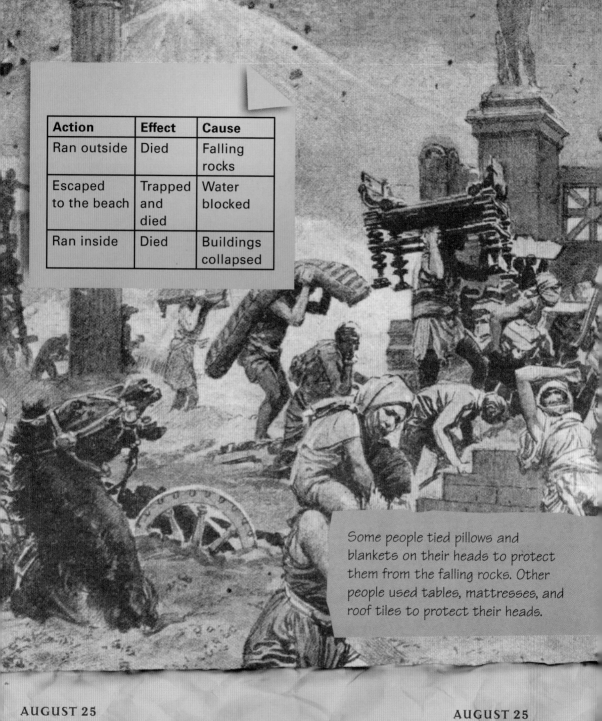

Action	Effect	Cause
Ran outside	Died	Falling rocks
Escaped to the beach	Trapped and died	Water blocked
Ran inside	Died	Buildings collapsed

Some people tied pillows and blankets on their heads to protect them from the falling rocks. Other people used tables, mattresses, and roof tiles to protect their heads.

AUGUST 25

1:00 A.M.

Surge 1 occurs. It travels at 60 mph. Its temperature is 1500 °F. The surge rushes into Herculaneum.

2:00–7:00 A.M.

Surges 2 and 3 occur. The surges hit the north wall of Pompeii.

7:00–8:00 A.M.

Surge 4 occurs. Pompeii is buried under seven feet of ash. Surges 5 and 6 occur for one hour.

AUGUST 25

9:00 A.M.

Eruption of Mount Vesuvius ends.

A young Roman writer had witnessed the eruption from Misenum. Misenum was 20 miles from Vesuvius, across the Bay of Naples. The writer's name was Pliny the Younger. He was 17 years old. Pliny was visiting his uncle, who was a writer and an **admiral** in the Roman navy. His uncle's name was Pliny the Elder. Pliny the Elder went by boat toward Mount Vesuvius to see if he could rescue a friend. However, the sea was wild and dangerous. Hot ash and floating pumice blocked his way. He was not able to get back. He died on the beach at Stabiae.

"a black and dreadful cloud"

Pliny the Younger wrote a letter to Tacitus, a historian of the day. He described the eruption. He also described the chaos that followed.

"like the darkness of a sealed room without lights"

"shrill cries of women"

"crying children"

"shouting men"

I know a boy named John Junior. His dad is named John Senior. I guess the Romans used *younger* and *elder* in a similar way that we use *junior* and *senior*. It really helps my understanding when I can make connections like this.

Pliny the Younger wrote about the huge cloud coming out of Mount Vesuvius. He said that it looked like an umbrella pine tree (left). Today, this kind of volcanic eruption is called a Plinian eruption (below).

Pompeii was lost under the ashes for more than 1,500 years. People forgot that a city had ever been there. Farmers grew olives and grapes in the **fertile** volcanic soil that formed from the ashes. Sometimes a farmer would find a brick or maybe even a statue in the ground. No one thought that these might have come from an ancient lost city.

In 1709, an Italian farmer was digging a well. He found beautiful marble statues. After that, people began digging in the area. They were looking for coins, jewelry, or anything valuable. Sometimes someone would find a skeleton. But no one was really interested in old bones. It wasn't until 1762 that people finally realized they had found the lost city of Pompeii.

This white marble statue of Eumachia is life-size. It was found in a building that some people believe was a slave market.

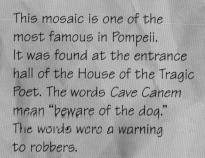

This mosaic is one of the most famous in Pompeii. It was found at the entrance hall of the House of the Tragic Poet. The words *Cave Canem* mean "beware of the dog." The words were a warning to robbers.

Inventory, 1762

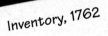

40 chandeliers

350 statues

700 painting fragments

700 vases

800 manuscripts

Not many small valuables were found at Pompeii. People probably took their valuables with them as they fled the city. This gold oil lamp is one of the most valuable objects found.

Whole buildings were destroyed when they were buried under the ash. Yet some delicate objects made of glass survived.

As more people heard about the discoveries at Pompeii, visitors came from all over the world. They watched the workers **excavate** the site. They crawled around among the ruins. They wanted to see some skeletons. They were hoping to find their own buried treasure. Many people took a bone or **artifact** home as a souvenir. Workers even used to arrange skulls and other bones to make them look more interesting to visitors.

In 1860, Giuseppe Fiorelli was put in charge of excavations at Pompeii. He thought the site should be guarded more closely. He knew that Pompeii would be ruined unless it was treated more carefully. He devised a new, scientific approach for recording what was uncovered at Pompeii.

Early 1900s

Fiorelli divided Pompeii into nine regions. Each region was given a Roman numeral. He subdivided these regions into 120 blocks. The blocks were called insulae. These were each given an Arabic numeral. Each house had an Arabic numeral too. Today, these numerals are often found on plaques at the front of the houses.

Giuseppe Fiorelli

	Region	Insula	House
The House of the Vettii	VI	15	1
The House of the Tragic Poet	VI	8	3
The House of Venus in the Shell	II	3	3

SHOCKER

In 1943, during World War II, the **Allies** dropped more than 160 bombs on Pompeii. They thought that German soldiers were hiding in the ruins.

Repairing damage, 1947

Parts of Pompeii were badly damaged by bombs during World War II. Luckily, 60 cases of artifacts had been removed from one site just days before it was destroyed. The bombings also unearthed previously undiscovered ruins.

Time Capsules

At the time of the eruption, more than 13 feet of ash buried the people and buildings of Pompeii. The ash that fell cooled, dried, and hardened. In time, the bodies that were trapped in the hardened ash rotted away. This left only bones inside the hard "bubbles." At first, workers simply crushed these ash bubbles to get at the bones inside.

In 1863, Fiorelli had an idea. He poured liquid plaster into these hollow spaces. The plaster dried in the shape of whoever or whatever had been buried by the ash. When the hard outer covering was chipped away, a human or animal form was revealed. He also used this method to reveal the shapes of shutters, doors, and furniture that had rotted away.

Many of the plaster casts reveal people's facial expressions as they died. Many victims suffered. Others look peaceful. They looked as if they had died while they slept. Sometimes families were found grouped together where they fell.

Pompeii, 1961

SHOCKER

One plaster cast showed a guard dog chained up. The dog couldn't escape. Another cast showed a slave. The slave was trying to take the iron bands off his ankles.

ASH GRAVES

The people die. Ten feet of ash and pumice cover them. The ash and pumice harden. The bodies rot away.

Centuries later, plaster is poured into the hollows.

The hard layer is chipped away. The plaster casts of bodies remain.

Many victims tried to protect their faces with a cloth or their clothes.

Giuseppe Fiorelli could not make a cast of every person who died in Pompeii. Only those who died on the second day, during the final blasts of hot ash, were covered by a hardened shell.

Making a Plaster Cast
1. Get some liquid plaster.
2. Pour into hollow spaces.
3. Wait for plaster to dry.
4. Chip away outer covering.

23

Skeletons, houses, and streets were not the only things found in the volcanic ash and mud of Pompeii. **Archaeologists** found many ordinary items. They found tables set for dinner. They found bowls of olives and jars of fruit. They discovered dishes, mirrors, and tools. Today, archaeologists can even figure out which plants grew in the Roman gardens.

Pompeii had about 35 bakeries. Most bakeries had about four **grindstones**. These were used to make flour. Mules turned the heavy grindstones. Bread was cooked in a brick oven for up to 45 minutes.

Many loaves of bread have been found in Pompeii. In one bakery, 81 loaves were discovered. They were overcooked!

Bread

Oven

Grindstone

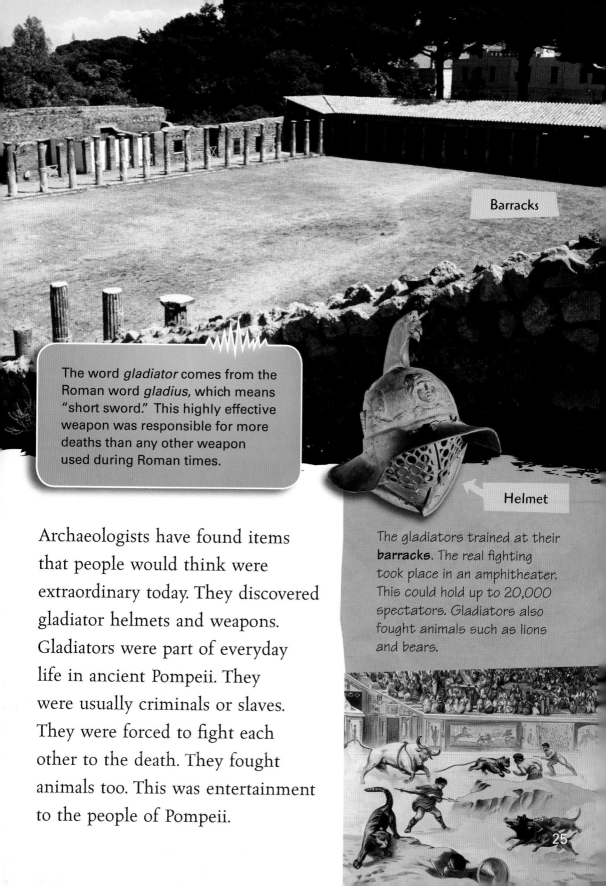

Barracks

The word *gladiator* comes from the Roman word *gladius*, which means "short sword." This highly effective weapon was responsible for more deaths than any other weapon used during Roman times.

Helmet

Archaeologists have found items that people would think were extraordinary today. They discovered gladiator helmets and weapons. Gladiators were part of everyday life in ancient Pompeii. They were usually criminals or slaves. They were forced to fight each other to the death. They fought animals too. This was entertainment to the people of Pompeii.

The gladiators trained at their **barracks**. The real fighting took place in an amphitheater. This could hold up to 20,000 spectators. Gladiators also fought animals such as lions and bears.

25

Nine miles away from Pompeii was the city of Herculaneum (*Hur kyuh LAY nee uhm*). It lay at the foot of Mount Vesuvius. It was also destroyed by the eruption. But, unlike Pompeii, Herculaneum was covered with volcanic mud. When the mud dried, it was as hard as rock. There were no ash bubbles. Only 32 bodies were found in the city. Archaeologists thought this meant that most of the people who lived there had been able to escape.

Layers of ash and pumice hit Pompeii. The weight of the fallout made many roofs collapse. However, in Herculaneum, volcanic mud hit the town. The hardened mud helped preserve many of the buildings.

Fallout at Herculaneum

82 feet

Fallout at Pompeii

13 feet

The volcanic blast at Herculaneum boiled people's brains. It also vaporized their skin in seconds!

Boat chamber

One boat storage chamber contained 40 skeletons. It also had the remains of a horse.

Then, in 1982, a new discovery made archaeologists change their minds. At the seashore near Herculaneum, they found more than 250 skeletons. It now seems likely that the people had run down to the sea to get away in their boats. Sadly, they arrived too late. Most of the dead were found in boat chambers by the water.

Archaeologists can tell a great deal from bones and teeth. The Ring Lady was found at Herculaneum. She was named for the two gold rings on her left hand. The Ring Lady was about 45 years old when she died. She had gum disease. However, she had no holes in her teeth!

27

The Secrets of Stabiae

There was another ancient Roman city destroyed by the Vesuvius eruption that buried Pompeii. The city was Stabiae. It lay three miles from Pompeii. The rich and powerful people of ancient Rome owned villas in Stabiae. The luxury villas overlooked the Bay of Naples. In August of 79 A.D., Stabiae was buried under about six feet of volcanic ash.

The ruins of Stabiae were discovered in 1749. Then, by 1782, Stabiae lay forgotten again. In the 1950s, a local high-school principal funded his own excavations at Stabiae. The principal was an avid historian. With two local helpers, he uncovered several luxurious ancient villas. Today, archaeologists are working to preserve them. They want to transform Stabiae into an archaeological park.

Computer reconstructions of Villa San Marco

I wasn't sure what the word *avid* meant. But then I reread the part about the principal funding his own excavations. It helped me understand that *avid* means "really interested". Sometimes rereading and thinking about what would make sense really helps.

People can now adopt a fresco at Stabiae. This helps raise money for excavation and preservation work.

It has been more than 200 years since the rediscovery of Pompeii. Today, three-quarters of Pompeii has been excavated. More than two million tourists visit Pompeii every year. Today, you can even take walking tours through Pompeii at night. However, the huge numbers of visitors are wearing it down. Many of the buildings are starting to crack and crumble. Some of the plaster casts are falling apart. Pollution is damaging everything, from stones to artwork.

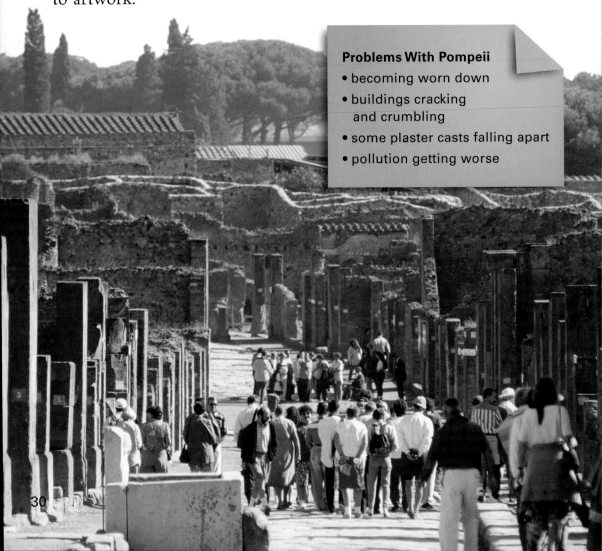

Problems With Pompeii
- becoming worn down
- buildings cracking and crumbling
- some plaster casts falling apart
- pollution getting worse

Mount Vesuvius is one of the world's most dangerous volcanoes. It has had a huge explosion of deadly gas and dust about every 200 years. The last eruption was in March 1944. It destroyed the village of San Sebastiano. Today, scientists study Vesuvius very closely.

1944

No one knows for sure what will happen to Pompeii. People all around the world are working together to save this important place. Even so, Vesuvius still stands in the distance. The volcano may stay quiet forever. Or it might send its deadly heat and ash to this ancient city once again.

DID YOU KNOW?

In 1997, Pompeii was listed as an **endangered** world monument by UNESCO. UNESCO stands for United Nations Educational, Scientific, and Cultural Organization.

In many places around the world, thousands of people live in the shadow of **active volcanoes**. **Volcanologists monitor** many volcanoes. They want to be able to evacuate people if they suspect a volcano is about to erupt. Italian scientists recently used computer **simulation** to estimate how many people would be affected if Mount Vesuvius erupted again.

WHAT DO YOU THINK?

Do you think it is a good idea for people to be allowed to live close to an active volcano?

PRO

The land around volcanoes is usually fertile. The people have lived and farmed areas around volcanoes for hundreds of years. They don't seem to worry about the risk. I think we should respect their decision to stay. The authorities should be able to give plenty of warning so that people can escape.

They have estimated that 300,000 people would be killed if the area were not evacuated in time. Authorities have to plan to evacuate more than half a million people living within a four-mile radius of Vesuvius. They say they would need a week's warning to be able to do this safely.

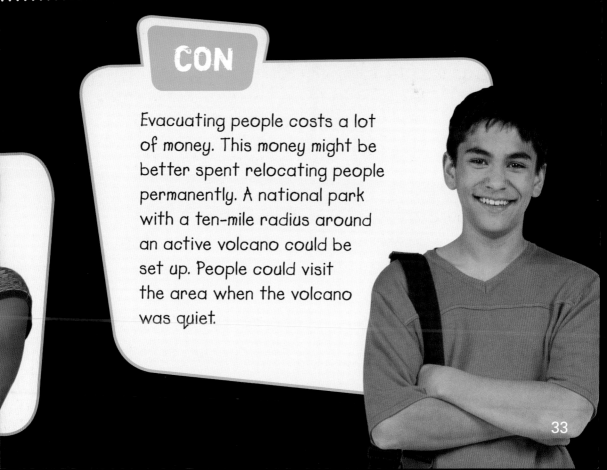

CON

Evacuating people costs a lot of money. This money might be better spent relocating people permanently. A national park with a ten-mile radius around an active volcano could be set up. People could visit the area when the volcano was quiet.

GLOSSARY

Amphitheater

active volcano a volcano that is currently erupting or is likely to do so in the future

admiral the highest rank in the navy

Allies (*AL eyes*) in World War II, the countries that fought on the side of Britain

amphitheater (*AM fi thee uh tur*) a large open-air building used for public events

barracks a large building that provides temporary housing for a group of people

debris (*duh BREE*) lots of small pieces of rock

endangered in danger of becoming one of the last left on Earth

eruption the bursting out of the ground of lava, rock, gases, or ash onto the earth's surface or into the air

evacuate (*e VAK yu ate*) to leave a place because it is too dangerous

fertile (*FUR tuhl*) full of nutrients that help plants grow

gladiator (*GLAD ee ay tur*) a person in ancient Rome who was trained to fight against an animal or another person

grindstone a flat, rotating stone used to crush something

monitor to keep watch over something. To monitor can involve taking measurements, such as temperature readings.

simulation (*sim yuh LAY shuhn*) the act of copying or imitating a natural event, such as a volcanic eruption, under experimental conditions using a computer

villa (*VIL uh*) a large house built around a central courtyard and garden

volcanologist a scientist who studies volcanoes

FIND OUT MORE

BOOKS

Deem, James M. *Bodies From the Ash*. Houghton Mifflin, 2005.

Harris, Nicholas. *Volcano*. Barron's Educational Series, 2001.

Lindeen, Mary. *Anatomy of a Volcano*. Scholastic Inc., 2008.

Pitt Kaplan, Sarah. *Pompeii: City of Ashes*. Children's Press, 2005.

Pope Osborne, Mary. *Pompeii: Lost and Found*. Knopf Books for Young Readers, 2006.

Roberts, Russell. *Mt. Vesuvius and the Destruction of Pompeii, A.D. 79.* Mitchell Lane Publishers, 2005.

WEB SITES

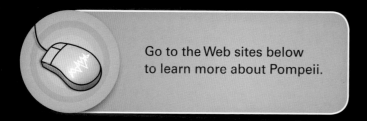

Go to the Web sites below to learn more about Pompeii.

www.dsc.discovery.com/convergence/pompeii/pompeii.html

www.awesomestories.com/disasters/pompeii/pompeii_ch1.htm

www.historyforkids.org/learn/romans/literature/elderpliny.htm

www.thehumorwriter.com/Kids_Corner_--_Original_Storie/Ancient_Pompeii/ancient_pompeii.html

INDEX

ABOUT THE AUTHOR

Mary Lindeen used to be a teacher, and now she writes books for kids. She especially likes to tell young readers about interesting places in the world and about things that happened a long time ago. Writing about Pompeii gave her a chance to do both: Italy is one of the most beautiful and interesting places in the world, and the city that was buried there by a volcanic eruption is a fascinating historical event.